WRITE

AND

RELEASE

JOURNAL

Let Go of
Worries and
Make Space
for Peace

WRITE

AND

RELEASE
JOURNAL

NICOLA RIES TAGGART

CHRONICLE BOOKS
SAN FRANCISCO

ISBN 978-1-7972-2754-2

Manufactured in China.

Design by Vanessa Dina.
Typesetting by Frank Brayton.

10 9 8 7 6 5 4 3 2 1

Chronicle Books publishes distinctive books and gifts. From award-winning children's titles, bestselling cookbooks, and eclectic pop culture to acclaimed works of art and design, stationery, and journals, we craft publishing that's instantly recognizable for its spirit and creativity. Enjoy our publishing and become part of our community at www.chroniclebooks.com.

Special quantity discounts are available to corporations and other organizations. Contact our premiums department at corporatesales@chroniclebooks.com or at 1-800-759-0190.

Chronicle Books LLC
680 Second Street
San Francisco, California 94107
www.chroniclebooks.com

INTRODUCTION

Welcome to *Write and Release Journal*, your companion for transforming your worries into wishes, seeing more positive perspectives and possibilities, and feeling more peace.

No one (and I mean *no one*) is immune to at least occasional challenges, concerns, and stress. I am a world-class worrier—one of my superpowers is to take any situation and create five different story lines for how it could go wrong. Living this way is not particularly positive or pleasant for me or for those around me, and, like many, I have a desire to worry less. I am guessing you might too, given that this journal is in your hands.

I have been a life and leadership coach for nearly twenty years, and during that time, I've worked with many clients to help them live in alignment with what's important to them, improve their work-life balance and well-being, and enhance their relationships. One thing I have learned is that the way in which we manage our challenges and stress has a significant impact on the way we feel, the way we show up, and the actions we take. Trying to ignore worries doesn't necessarily help us move on. In fact, the more we dismiss or deny them, the louder they might get and the more they might distract us from being or doing our best.

In this journal, you'll find a simple practice for shifting the relationship you have with your worries by naming and then releasing them. No matter the source of your concerns, releasing worries creates some much-needed space in your mind. Over the years, I have experienced the magic of applying this journaling technique in my own life and in the lives of my coaching clients. Using this practice, a client of mine who felt worried and disappointed about a job loss learned to shift their energy toward excitement about their career direction and next ideal job situation. They were able to find motivation and feel progress in their search, which eventually led to a new job. Another client who was worried and discouraged about disconnection in a romantic relationship was able to use this method to be more intentional in their actions and conversations. By engaging with these journaling prompts, they became more open and vulnerable and fostered communication that created greater connection and intimacy in their relationship.

These are just a couple of the many stories I could share about this transformative journaling practice. And while I know we cannot eliminate all our worries, the feelings of peace and contentment that come from learning how to better manage what's on our mind (by releasing rather than ruminating) are key to living a happier and healthier life.

This is why I am excited that the *Write and Release Journal* has found its way to you. It's a simple yet highly effective tool for helping you turn your worries into wishes so that you can stress less and shine more.

Nicola

NICOLA RIES TAGGART
Author of *Calm the Chaos Journal* and *Calm the Chaos Cards*
Life and leadership success strategist and coach

This tool was created with several therapeutic and coaching techniques in mind: expressive writing, designating a scheduled time to worry, naming our emotions, and imagining that things could work out for the best instead of for the worst. Practicing these four techniques has been proven to help people feel more calm and joy by decreasing stress and anxiety, increasing positivity and perspective, and improving sleep and focus. In addition to the writing pages, you'll also find encouraging affirmations sprinkled throughout to help spark your courage, confidence, and clarity as you put pen to paper and consider these repeating journaling prompts:

WRITE IT

What's on your mind? What issue(s) (big or small) are you worried about right now? What thoughts are weighing you down or distracting you?

The purpose of this section is to give voice to what is on your mind. It's a place to get the thoughts and worries out of your head (and heart) and down on paper so that you can identify and acknowledge them.

RELEASE IT

How can you shift your perspective? Where is there hope and possibility related to the issue(s) you are worried about right now? What are some positive things that have or could come from this?

The purpose of this section is to shift your focus from your concerns and worries of what did or could go wrong to what is going and could go right, and to help you find a new perspective or new possibilities that allow you to let go of what's not in your control and get clarity around what is.

The difference between a worry and a wish is simply where you choose to put your focus. In the first step, by writing down your thoughts, you give yourself permission to actively pay attention to your worries. But in this second step, you will intentionally shift your attention and release those concerns by focusing on better-feeling thoughts.

This two-part process allows you to manage stress and anxiety and then shift your perspective to invite greater feelings of positivity and peace. There is no right or wrong way to engage with these prompts. You could create a bulleted list, draw out a map of what's going on in your mind, sketch how you feel, do a brain dump of all your current anxieties, or write in stream of consciousness—experiment with what works for you. What matters the most is that you choose a way that allows you to put in writing what you are thinking (and feeling) in the easiest and most helpful way possible. Here are a few examples to help inspire your process:

Example 1

WRITE IT

What's on your mind? What issue(s) (big or small) are you worried about right now? What thoughts are weighing you down or distracting you?

- Sam's friendships and the way kids blew him off today
- I worry he feels alone, and I don't know how to help!

- What if he doesn't find a circle of friends?
- Will this affect him in high school?
- Could it be him? Is he annoying? Or are they just mean?
- Is something wrong with my son?
- Imagining him walking home alone makes me want to cry

RELEASE IT

How can you shift your perspective? Where is there hope and possibility related to the issue(s) you are worried about right now? What are some positive things that have or could come from this?

I want Sam to feel good about his friendships. I want him to feel like he belongs and like he's got a small circle of friends that he feels connected to. I want him to feel confident and happy. I want him to have a positive social experience this year and create some really positive relationships next year when he goes to high school. Ultimately, I just want him to be happy and healthy. I realize that I can't do anything to make this happen for him. All we can do is be there to listen to him, support him, and encourage him to reach out to other kids to connect. I have to remember that he gets lots of social connection at school and on his sports teams. I also feel grateful that he chose to tell us about what happened and how he was feeling instead of holding it in. Maybe we can encourage him to invite a new friend over each week to strengthen those one-on-one relationships. I know nothing is wrong with him. He's a great kid. This is normal. Kids go through this in middle school all the time. Maybe this experience will help him figure out what kind of friend he wants to be and what kind of friends he wants. This could even end up being positive in his development!

Example 2

WRITE IT

What's on your mind? What issue(s) (big or small) are you worried about right now? What thoughts are weighing you down or distracting you?

RELEASE IT

How can you shift your perspective? Where is there hope and possibility related to the issue(s) you are worried about right now? What are some positive things that have or could come from this?

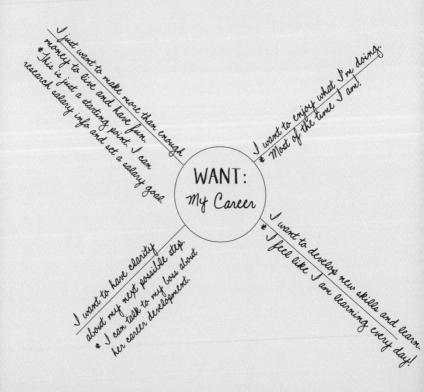

I just want to make more than enough money to live and have fun.
* This is just a starting point. I can research salary info and set a salary goal.

I want to enjoy what I'm doing.
* Most of the time I am.

WANT:
My Career

I want to have clarity about my next possible step.
* I can talk to my boss about her career development.

I want to develop new skills and learn.
* I feel like I am learning every day!

I WILL FOCUS ON WHAT I CAN CONTROL AND LET GO OF WHAT I CANNOT.

When you try to control what you cannot, it causes stress and anxiety. Surrendering to what you can't control and focusing on what you can brings great peace.

WRITE IT

What's on your mind? What issue(s) (big or small) are you
worried about right now? What thoughts are weighing
you down or distracting you?

_____

_____

_____

_____

_____

_____

_____

_____

_____

_____

_____

_____

_____

_____

_____

RELEASE IT

How can you shift your perspective? Where is there hope and possibility related to the issue(s) you are worried about right now? What are some positive things that have or could come from this?

_____

_____

_____

_____

_____

_____

_____

_____

_____

_____

_____

_____

_____

_____

_____

WRITE IT

What's on your mind? What issue(s) (big or small) are you
worried about right now? What thoughts are weighing
you down or distracting you?

_____

_____

_____

_____

_____

_____

_____

_____

_____

_____

_____

_____

_____

_____

_____

_____

_____

_____

RELEASE IT

How can you shift your perspective? Where is there hope and possibility related to the issue(s) you are worried about right now? What are some positive things that have or could come from this?

_____

_____

_____

_____

_____

_____

_____

_____

_____

_____

_____

_____

_____

_____

_____

_____

_____

I CAN CULTIVATE CALM BY EMBRACING THE PRESENT MOMENT.

You experience stress when you are mired in the past or worried about the future. Stressing over things that are finished or that haven't yet happened wastes your energy on that which you can't control. All you have is this moment. And this moment contains all that you need.

WRITE IT

What's on your mind? What issue(s) (big or small) are you
worried about right now? What thoughts are weighing
you down or distracting you?

_____

_____

_____

_____

_____

_____

_____

_____

_____

_____

_____

_____

_____

_____

RELEASE IT

How can you shift your perspective? Where is there hope
and possibility related to the issue(s) you are worried about
right now? What are some positive things that have or
could come from this?

_____

_____

_____

_____

_____

_____

_____

_____

_____

_____

_____

_____

_____

_____

_____

I WILL
LET
GRATITUDE
BECOME
MY
FOUNDATION.

Gratitude is an endless resource that is always at your disposal when you need it. Naming the things you're grateful for can pull you out of dark moments and break unhealthy thought cycles.

WRITE IT

What's on your mind? What issue(s) (big or small) are you worried about right now? What thoughts are weighing you down or distracting you?

_____

_____

_____

_____

_____

_____

_____

_____

_____

_____

_____

_____

_____

_____

RELEASE IT

How can you shift your perspective? Where is there hope and possibility related to the issue(s) you are worried about right now? What are some positive things that have or could come from this?

_____

_____

_____

_____

_____

_____

_____

_____

_____

_____

_____

_____

_____

_____

_____

_____

I
CAN
WALK
AWAY.

Sometimes the best thing you can do is walk away from a situation that no longer serves you. Walking away is not the same thing as giving up. Sometimes the most loving thing you can do for yourself is to stop clinging to things that are not meant to be or no longer serve you.

WRITE IT

What's on your mind? What issue(s) (big or small) are you
worried about right now? What thoughts are weighing
you down or distracting you?

_____

_____

_____

_____

_____

_____

_____

_____

_____

_____

_____

_____

_____

_____

_____

_____

RELEASE IT

How can you shift your perspective? Where is there hope and possibility related to the issue(s) you are worried about right now? What are some positive things that have or could come from this?

_____

_____

_____

_____

_____

_____

_____

_____

_____

_____

_____

_____

_____

_____

WRITE IT

What's on your mind? What issue(s) (big or small) are you
worried about right now? What thoughts are weighing
you down or distracting you?

_____

_____

_____

_____

_____

_____

_____

_____

_____

_____

_____

_____

_____

_____

_____

RELEASE IT

How can you shift your perspective? Where is there hope and possibility related to the issue(s) you are worried about right now? What are some positive things that have or could come from this?

_____

_____

_____

_____

_____

_____

_____

_____

_____

_____

_____

_____

_____

_____

_____

_____

I
CLAIM
CALM
AS MY
SUPERPOWER.

Even when stress is swirling around, you don't have to operate from a place of drama and distraction by overfocusing on your worries. You can choose calm as your point of power and direct your mind to more positive perspectives and possibilities.

WRITE IT

What's on your mind? What issue(s) (big or small) are you
worried about right now? What thoughts are weighing
you down or distracting you?

_____

_____

_____

_____

_____

_____

_____

_____

_____

_____

_____

_____

_____

_____

_____

_____

_____

RELEASE IT

How can you shift your perspective? Where is there hope
and possibility related to the issue(s) you are worried about
right now? What are some positive things that have or
could come from this?

_____

_____

_____

_____

_____

_____

_____

_____

_____

_____

_____

_____

_____

_____

_____

WRITE IT

What's on your mind? What issue(s) (big or small) are you
worried about right now? What thoughts are weighing
you down or distracting you?

_____

_____

_____

_____

_____

_____

_____

_____

_____

_____

_____

_____

_____

_____

_____

RELEASE IT

How can you shift your perspective? Where is there hope
and possibility related to the issue(s) you are worried about
right now? What are some positive things that have or
could come from this?

_____

_____

_____

_____

_____

_____

_____

_____

_____

_____

_____

_____

_____

_____

_____

_____

_____

_____

I GET TO
DECIDE
WHERE
I GIVE MY
TIME AND
ATTENTION.

Be intentional about where you focus your thoughts, words, and actions. Give yourself some time to process your worries, and then choose to shift your focus toward clarifying what you want, sharing what you need, and taking action to support those things.

WRITE IT

What's on your mind? What issue(s) (big or small) are you
worried about right now? What thoughts are weighing
you down or distracting you?

_____

_____

_____

_____

_____

_____

_____

_____

_____

_____

_____

_____

_____

_____

_____

_____

_____

_____

RELEASE IT

How can you shift your perspective? Where is there hope and possibility related to the issue(s) you are worried about right now? What are some positive things that have or could come from this?

_____

_____

_____

_____

_____

_____

_____

_____

_____

_____

_____

_____

_____

_____

_____

_____

_____

_____

WORRIES
PREVENT
MY LIGHT
FROM
SHINING
BRIGHT.

When you let your worries run wild, they keep you distracted and diminish your energy and presence. Making time to write down and acknowledge your concerns allows you to release them and create space to shine bigger and brighter.

WRITE IT

What's on your mind? What issue(s) (big or small) are you worried about right now? What thoughts are weighing you down or distracting you?

_____

_____

_____

_____

_____

_____

_____

_____

_____

_____

_____

_____

_____

_____

_____

_____

_____

RELEASE IT

How can you shift your perspective? Where is there hope and possibility related to the issue(s) you are worried about right now? What are some positive things that have or could come from this?

_____

_____

_____

_____

_____

_____

_____

_____

_____

_____

_____

_____

_____

_____

_____

WRITE IT

What's on your mind? What issue(s) (big or small) are you
worried about right now? What thoughts are weighing
you down or distracting you?

_____

_____

_____

_____

_____

_____

_____

_____

_____

_____

_____

_____

_____

_____

_____

RELEASE IT

How can you shift your perspective? Where is there hope and possibility related to the issue(s) you are worried about right now? What are some positive things that have or could come from this?

_____

_____

_____

_____

_____

_____

_____

_____

_____

_____

_____

_____

_____

_____

_____

_____

_____

ALL

IS

WELL.

Your individual perspective is too limited to see all the things happening that are bigger than you. Being too closely attached to a particular problem or worry narrows your energy and perspective. Even in the chaos of the moment, know that there is still joy, beauty, and kindness surrounding you.

WRITE IT

What's on your mind? What issue(s) (big or small) are you worried about right now? What thoughts are weighing you down or distracting you?

_____

_____

_____

_____

_____

_____

_____

_____

_____

_____

_____

_____

_____

_____

_____

_____

_____

RELEASE IT

How can you shift your perspective? Where is there hope
and possibility related to the issue(s) you are worried about
right now? What are some positive things that have or
could come from this?

_____

_____

_____

_____

_____

_____

_____

_____

_____

_____

_____

_____

_____

_____

_____

_____

EVEN
IN THE
MIDST OF
STRESS,
I CAN FIND
HOPE.

When you are feeling overwhelmed, it can take extra effort to tap into hope. But no matter what is happening, you can always access gratitude and look for small blessings to transform your experience and shift your perspective.

WRITE IT

What's on your mind? What issue(s) (big or small) are you worried about right now? What thoughts are weighing you down or distracting you?

_____

_____

_____

_____

_____

_____

_____

_____

_____

_____

_____

_____

_____

_____

_____

_____

_____

_____

RELEASE IT

How can you shift your perspective? Where is there hope
and possibility related to the issue(s) you are worried about
right now? What are some positive things that have or
could come from this?

_____

_____

_____

_____

_____

_____

_____

_____

_____

_____

_____

_____

_____

_____

_____

_____

_____

THERE'S A
QUIET SPACE
IN MY HEART
THAT ALWAYS
KNOWS
WHAT'S
IMPORTANT.

It's easy to get tangled up with external stressors and internal worry. But deep in your heart, there is calm and clarity that you can always tap into to point you in a more positive and peaceful direction.

WRITE IT

What's on your mind? What issue(s) (big or small) are you
worried about right now? What thoughts are weighing
you down or distracting you?

_____

_____

_____

_____

_____

_____

_____

_____

_____

_____

_____

_____

_____

_____

_____

_____

RELEASE IT

How can you shift your perspective? Where is there hope and possibility related to the issue(s) you are worried about right now? What are some positive things that have or could come from this?

_____

_____

_____

_____

_____

_____

_____

_____

_____

_____

_____

_____

_____

_____

_____

_____

WRITE IT

What's on your mind? What issue(s) (big or small) are you
worried about right now? What thoughts are weighing
you down or distracting you?

_____

_____

_____

_____

_____

_____

_____

_____

_____

_____

_____

_____

_____

_____

_____

_____

_____

RELEASE IT

How can you shift your perspective? Where is there hope and possibility related to the issue(s) you are worried about right now? What are some positive things that have or could come from this?

_____

_____

_____

_____

_____

_____

_____

_____

_____

_____

_____

_____

_____

_____

_____

TAKE
IT
MOMENT
BY
MOMENT.

Worrying about the future can be overwhelming and send you down a spiral of unnecessary stress. Focus on what is right in front of you at this moment and take it one step at a time. Trust that one step will guide you to the next, and then the next, and then the next.

WRITE IT

What's on your mind? What issue(s) (big or small) are you
worried about right now? What thoughts are weighing
you down or distracting you?

_____

_____

_____

_____

_____

_____

_____

_____

_____

_____

_____

_____

_____

_____

_____

_____

_____

RELEASE IT

How can you shift your perspective? Where is there hope and possibility related to the issue(s) you are worried about right now? What are some positive things that have or could come from this?

_____

_____

_____

_____

_____

_____

_____

_____

_____

_____

_____

_____

_____

_____

_____

WRITE IT

What's on your mind? What issue(s) (big or small) are you worried about right now? What thoughts are weighing you down or distracting you?

_____

_____

_____

_____

_____

_____

_____

_____

_____

_____

_____

_____

_____

_____

RELEASE IT

How can you shift your perspective? Where is there hope and possibility related to the issue(s) you are worried about right now? What are some positive things that have or could come from this?

_____

_____

_____

_____

_____

_____

_____

_____

_____

_____

_____

_____

_____

_____

_____

_____

_____

MY

MIND

IS A

POWERFUL

TOOL.

Focusing on what you don't want to happen is a habit that hinders your inner peace. By acknowledging the worry and then shifting your focus toward what is good, what you are grateful for, and what you want to create, you stop the thought patterns that hold you back.

WRITE IT

What's on your mind? What issue(s) (big or small) are you
worried about right now? What thoughts are weighing
you down or distracting you?

_____

_____

_____

_____

_____

_____

_____

_____

_____

_____

_____

_____

_____

_____

_____

_____

_____

RELEASE IT

How can you shift your perspective? Where is there hope
and possibility related to the issue(s) you are worried about
right now? What are some positive things that have or
could come from this?

_____

_____

_____

_____

_____

_____

_____

_____

_____

_____

_____

_____

_____

_____

_____

_____

WRITE IT

What's on your mind? What issue(s) (big or small) are you
worried about right now? What thoughts are weighing
you down or distracting you?

_____

_____

_____

_____

_____

_____

_____

_____

_____

_____

_____

_____

_____

_____

_____

_____

RELEASE IT

How can you shift your perspective? Where is there hope and possibility related to the issue(s) you are worried about right now? What are some positive things that have or could come from this?

_____

_____

_____

_____

_____

_____

_____

_____

_____

_____

_____

_____

_____

_____

_____

_____

_____

IT'S NOT MY JOB TO MANAGE EVERYTHING FOR EVERYONE ELSE.

Attempting to manage things that are not your responsibility leads to unnecessary stress. As you note your worries, ask yourself if this worry is yours to own. If it belongs to someone else, release it by letting go and offering love for the person whose responsibility it is.

WRITE IT

What's on your mind? What issue(s) (big or small) are you
worried about right now? What thoughts are weighing
you down or distracting you?

_____

_____

_____

_____

_____

_____

_____

_____

_____

_____

_____

_____

_____

_____

_____

_____

_____

RELEASE IT

How can you shift your perspective? Where is there hope
and possibility related to the issue(s) you are worried about
right now? What are some positive things that have or
could come from this?

_____

_____

_____

_____

_____

_____

_____

_____

_____

_____

_____

_____

_____

_____

_____

_____

WHEN
I ALIGN MY
THOUGHTS,
WORDS, AND
ACTIONS,
MAGIC
HAPPENS.

You have control over the three most important things in your life: what you think, what you say, and what you do. Clarify what you want for yourself, share what you want (rather than what you don't want) with others, and act from a positive and empowered place.

WRITE IT

What's on your mind? What issue(s) (big or small) are you worried about right now? What thoughts are weighing you down or distracting you?

_____

_____

_____

_____

_____

_____

_____

_____

_____

_____

_____

_____

_____

_____

_____

RELEASE IT

How can you shift your perspective? Where is there hope
and possibility related to the issue(s) you are worried about
right now? What are some positive things that have or
could come from this?

_____

_____

_____

_____

_____

_____

_____

_____

_____

_____

_____

_____

_____

_____

_____

I

CHOOSE

CALM

OVER

CHAOS.

Worrying keeps your mind and body in a state of stress and chaos. Choosing to consciously calm your mind by shifting your worries into wishes is an act of love for yourself and for others that will set you free.

WRITE IT

What's on your mind? What issue(s) (big or small) are you
worried about right now? What thoughts are weighing
you down or distracting you?

_____

_____

_____

_____

_____

_____

_____

_____

_____

_____

_____

_____

_____

_____

_____

_____

RELEASE IT

How can you shift your perspective? Where is there hope
and possibility related to the issue(s) you are worried about
right now? What are some positive things that have or
could come from this?

_____

_____

_____

_____

_____

_____

_____

_____

_____

_____

_____

_____

_____

_____

_____

_____

WRITE IT

What's on your mind? What issue(s) (big or small) are you worried about right now? What thoughts are weighing you down or distracting you?

_____

_____

_____

_____

_____

_____

_____

_____

_____

_____

_____

_____

_____

_____

_____

_____

_____

RELEASE IT

How can you shift your perspective? Where is there hope and possibility related to the issue(s) you are worried about right now? What are some positive things that have or could come from this?

_____

_____

_____

_____

_____

_____

_____

_____

_____

_____

_____

_____

_____

_____

_____

_____

_____

THERE
IS
POWER
IN
THE
SILENCE.

When you slow down and let your mind be still, you invite calm and clarity. Use this sacred silent time to feel the fear, acknowledge the worries, and welcome the wishes.

WRITE IT

What's on your mind? What issue(s) (big or small) are you
worried about right now? What thoughts are weighing
you down or distracting you?

_____

_____

_____

_____

_____

_____

_____

_____

_____

_____

_____

_____

_____

_____

_____

RELEASE IT

How can you shift your perspective? Where is there hope and possibility related to the issue(s) you are worried about right now? What are some positive things that have or could come from this?

_____

_____

_____

_____

_____

_____

_____

_____

_____

_____

_____

_____

_____

_____

_____

_____

I AM
THE
PEACEKEEPER
OF MY
INNER
WORLD.

As the director of your thoughts, protector of your feelings, and leader of your actions, you determine the level of inner peace you experience.

WRITE IT

What's on your mind? What issue(s) (big or small) are you worried about right now? What thoughts are weighing you down or distracting you?

_____

_____

_____

_____

_____

_____

_____

_____

_____

_____

_____

_____

_____

_____

_____

_____

_____

RELEASE IT

How can you shift your perspective? Where is there hope
and possibility related to the issue(s) you are worried about
right now? What are some positive things that have or
could come from this?

_____

_____

_____

_____

_____

_____

_____

_____

_____

_____

_____

_____

_____

_____

_____

_____

_____

WRITE IT

What's on your mind? What issue(s) (big or small) are you worried about right now? What thoughts are weighing you down or distracting you?

_____

_____

_____

_____

_____

_____

_____

_____

_____

_____

_____

_____

_____

_____

_____

_____

_____

RELEASE IT

How can you shift your perspective? Where is there hope
and possibility related to the issue(s) you are worried about
right now? What are some positive things that have or
could come from this?

_____

_____

_____

_____

_____

_____

_____

_____

_____

_____

_____

_____

_____

_____

_____

_____

_____

THINGS
ARE
ALWAYS
WORKING
OUT.

When life isn't looking the way you want it to, it's easy for the worries to kick in. But trusting that life is moving in the right direction will give you enormous power. Remind yourself that even if you can't see it in the moment, there is always positivity and possibility around you.

WRITE IT

What's on your mind? What issue(s) (big or small) are you worried about right now? What thoughts are weighing you down or distracting you?

_____

_____

_____

_____

_____

_____

_____

_____

_____

_____

_____

_____

_____

_____

_____

_____

RELEASE IT

How can you shift your perspective? Where is there hope
and possibility related to the issue(s) you are worried about
right now? What are some positive things that have or
could come from this?

_____

_____

_____

_____

_____

_____

_____

_____

_____

_____

_____

_____

_____

_____

_____

_____

_____

MIRACLES HAPPEN EVERY DAY.

In this crazy and chaotic world, it's easy to focus on what's wrong or what could go wrong. But wondrous things are always unfolding all around you, in every moment of every day. Keep your eyes and heart open to what's possible, and refocus on the beauty and good in the world.

WRITE IT

What's on your mind? What issue(s) (big or small) are you
worried about right now? What thoughts are weighing
you down or distracting you?

_____

_____

_____

_____

_____

_____

_____

_____

_____

_____

_____

_____

_____

_____

_____

_____

RELEASE IT

How can you shift your perspective? Where is there hope and possibility related to the issue(s) you are worried about right now? What are some positive things that have or could come from this?

_____

_____

_____

_____

_____

_____

_____

_____

_____

_____

_____

_____

_____

_____

_____

_____

_____

WRITE IT

What's on your mind? What issue(s) (big or small) are you
worried about right now? What thoughts are weighing
you down or distracting you?

_____

_____

_____

_____

_____

_____

_____

_____

_____

_____

_____

_____

_____

_____

_____

DATE:

RELEASE IT

How can you shift your perspective? Where is there hope
and possibility related to the issue(s) you are worried about
right now? What are some positive things that have or
could come from this?

_____

_____

_____

_____

_____

_____

_____

_____

_____

_____

_____

_____

_____

_____

_____

_____

_____

THE THOUGHTS I CHOOSE SHAPE MY EXPERIENCE.

Every moment you have a choice about what you focus on. Some thoughts are conscious; many are not. With each thought, you shape the experience of your life. In order to create a calmer, more peaceful experience, choose thoughts that support this intention.

WRITE IT

What's on your mind? What issue(s) (big or small) are you
worried about right now? What thoughts are weighing
you down or distracting you?

_____

_____

_____

_____

_____

_____

_____

_____

_____

_____

_____

_____

_____

_____

_____

RELEASE IT

How can you shift your perspective? Where is there hope and possibility related to the issue(s) you are worried about right now? What are some positive things that have or could come from this?

_____

_____

_____

_____

_____

_____

_____

_____

_____

_____

_____

_____

_____

_____

_____

_____

MY
LIFE
IS MY
OWN
TO
CREATE.

Energy flows where your focus goes—this means that you are creating your life from the thoughts you give the most attention. Are you creating life from fear and worries? Or from peace and possibilities? Intentionally turn your focus more toward what you want and less toward what you don't.

WRITE IT

What's on your mind? What issue(s) (big or small) are you
worried about right now? What thoughts are weighing
you down or distracting you?

_____

_____

_____

_____

_____

_____

_____

_____

_____

_____

_____

_____

_____

_____

_____

RELEASE IT

How can you shift your perspective? Where is there hope and possibility related to the issue(s) you are worried about right now? What are some positive things that have or could come from this?

_____

_____

_____

_____

_____

_____

_____

_____

_____

_____

_____

_____

_____

_____

_____

_____

WRITE IT

What's on your mind? What issue(s) (big or small) are you
worried about right now? What thoughts are weighing
you down or distracting you?

_____

_____

_____

_____

_____

_____

_____

_____

_____

_____

_____

_____

_____

_____

_____

_____

RELEASE IT

How can you shift your perspective? Where is there hope and possibility related to the issue(s) you are worried about right now? What are some positive things that have or could come from this?

_____

_____

_____

_____

_____

_____

_____

_____

_____

_____

_____

_____

_____

_____

_____

I AM
RESPONSIBLE
FOR THE
ATTITUDE
I BRING
TO EACH
SITUATION.

You cannot control many of the things that happen around you and to you, but you have 100 percent control over what you focus on and your attitude toward each situation. Bringing your attention to the power you have over your energy will profoundly affect the way you move through your day.

WRITE IT

What's on your mind? What issue(s) (big or small) are you worried about right now? What thoughts are weighing you down or distracting you?

_____

_____

_____

_____

_____

_____

_____

_____

_____

_____

_____

_____

_____

_____

_____

_____

RELEASE IT

How can you shift your perspective? Where is there hope and possibility related to the issue(s) you are worried about right now? What are some positive things that have or could come from this?

_____

_____

_____

_____

_____

_____

_____

_____

_____

_____

_____

_____

_____

_____

_____

WRITE IT

What's on your mind? What issue(s) (big or small) are you
worried about right now? What thoughts are weighing
you down or distracting you?

_____

_____

_____

_____

_____

_____

_____

_____

_____

_____

_____

_____

_____

_____

_____

RELEASE IT

How can you shift your perspective? Where is there hope and possibility related to the issue(s) you are worried about right now? What are some positive things that have or could come from this?

_____

_____

_____

_____

_____

_____

_____

_____

_____

_____

_____

_____

_____

_____

_____

_____

_____

I CAN

FEEL

MY WAY

TOWARD

CLARITY.

Being confused can cause a lot of stress. When something feels overwhelming, trying too hard to figure it out in your head might make it even worse. Get out of your head and get into your heart by imagining how it would feel if everything worked out. Tap into that feeling and make space for a solution or path to unfold.

WRITE IT

What's on your mind? What issue(s) (big or small) are you worried about right now? What thoughts are weighing you down or distracting you?

_____

_____

_____

_____

_____

_____

_____

_____

_____

_____

_____

_____

_____

_____

_____

_____

_____

RELEASE IT

How can you shift your perspective? Where is there hope and possibility related to the issue(s) you are worried about right now? What are some positive things that have or could come from this?

_____

_____

_____

_____

_____

_____

_____

_____

_____

_____

_____

_____

_____

_____

_____

_____

_____

_____

I

EMBRACE

MY

WISE

ONE

WITHIN.

There is so much wisdom within you, but it can often be drowned out by worries and stress. Make time to listen. Your inner wisdom waits for your attention, ready to support and guide you when you need it.

WRITE IT

What's on your mind? What issue(s) (big or small) are you
worried about right now? What thoughts are weighing
you down or distracting you?

_____

_____

_____

_____

_____

_____

_____

_____

_____

_____

_____

_____

_____

_____

_____

_____

_____

_____

RELEASE IT

How can you shift your perspective? Where is there hope and possibility related to the issue(s) you are worried about right now? What are some positive things that have or could come from this?

_____

_____

_____

_____

_____

_____

_____

_____

_____

_____

_____

_____

_____

_____

_____

WRITE IT

What's on your mind? What issue(s) (big or small) are you
worried about right now? What thoughts are weighing
you down or distracting you?

_____

_____

_____

_____

_____

_____

_____

_____

_____

_____

_____

_____

_____

_____

_____

_____

_____

RELEASE IT

How can you shift your perspective? Where is there hope and possibility related to the issue(s) you are worried about right now? What are some positive things that have or could come from this?

_____

_____

_____

_____

_____

_____

_____

_____

_____

_____

_____

_____

_____

_____

_____

_____

I

AM

HERE:
LIVING,

BREATHING,

AND

ALIVE.